THE
TOP STEP

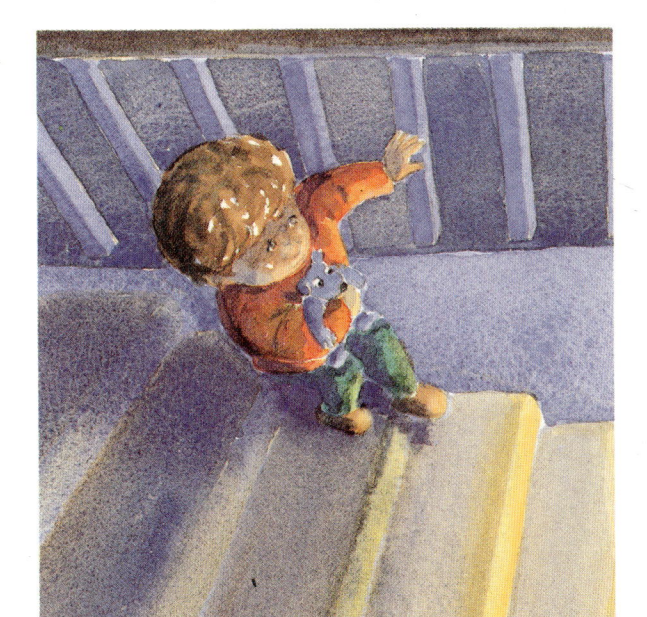

Written by Mike Torbe
Illustrated by Kaoru Miyake

Collins Educational
An imprint of HarperCollins*Publishers*

"Bernie," Ian whispered to his cuddly blue dog. "There's a Something there in the dark." Bernie didn't answer, but stared bravely ahead, as he always did when they went up to bed together.

Ian and Bernie stood on the step below the landing. Behind them was the downstairs light, but in front were dark shadows.

"Something's waiting there," Ian whispered. Bernie rustled quietly as Ian gripped him hard. They both knew they must not put a foot on the top step, because then the Something would come and get them.

"I think I'm thirsty," said Ian. "Let's go and get a drink." So he and Bernie went downstairs again, to the room where his parents were talking, and where it was bright and warm.

The next night, Ian and Bernie did not go upstairs on their own, but were carried up. When they were in bed, Ian hid under the duvet with Bernie, so that Bernie wouldn't feel alone and frightened. For a few days they both avoided the top step.

She stroked Bernie's head, and straightened the right ear, the floppy one that always hung down.

"I'm going to tell Bernie a secret magic word, and if he ever thinks there's something awful in the dark, all he has to do is to think of that word.

"The very second he thinks of this secret word, all the bad things will be gone." And then she whispered, very, very quietly in Bernie's ear.

"Bernie might forget it," said Dad. "If Ian knew the word as well, he could remind Bernie of it when he forgets."
"What do you think?" said Mum. "Could you remember it? And could you keep it really secret?" Ian nodded.

Mum leant forward, and whispered the word very, very quietly in Ian's ear. "Now you know it too," she said. "And I suppose if you think of it first, the bad things will be gone even before Bernie knows it."

Bernie and Ian walked up to bed that night, and Dad came with them. When they were tucked into bed together, Ian said, "Dad, Bernie is lucky to have someone to look after him, isn't he?"

"Oh yes," said Dad. "He's very lucky, indeed."
He kissed both of them good night, and went downstairs.